D0845647

JoSon

JoSon

Graphis, Inc.
114 West 17th Street, Second Floor
New York, NY 10011
United States of America
www.graphis.com

Designed by B. Martin Pedersen & Jimin Nam
Edited by Arthur Huang

© 2003 Graphis, Inc. All rights reserved. No part of this publication may be
reproduced or transmitted in any form or by any means, electronic, photocopying, recording,
or otherwise, without the prior written permission of Graphis, Inc.

First published in June 2013
ISBN: 978-1-932026-84-9

Graphis

Contents

Throughout history, our fascination with flowers has inspired us to preserve them through art. Dynasties in the ancient civilizations of Crete, China and Egypt all expected their artisans to depict flowers in paint, or clay, or gold, while monks copying illustrations from the Roman Empire through the Renaissance offered readers a catalogue of useful plants. In the 1700s, improved tools for collecting and examining flowers at close range gave us an age of still-lifes from the Netherlands and decades of magnificent folios in books we call florilegia. By the 18th and 19th centuries horticulture became art, and art served science.

What you are holding in your hands is both an evolution and a continuation of this great tradition. It may seem ironic, but the technology of fiber optics, macro lenses and the digitized camera gives us much the same detail and depth of focus that drawing and coloring by hand gave us until well into the 20th century. Nothing will ever replace the meticulous, hand-painted studio flower, but joSon's techniques give us in electrons the same beauty and detail accomplished in brushstrokes. He takes the same delight in depicting the long, sigmoid or coiled stems that attach the flowers to the parent plant as the Victorian painters of

orchids did, and his wonder and respect for the sheer architecture of flowers on stems is a visual throwback to the 1700's, when Linnaeus classified the natural architecture of flowering branches. He seems fascinated by two self-repeating, flowering stems in nature. First, he likes the flowering stem Linnaeus, called the head or involucrum. Here, small flowers (florets) massed together on a flat-headed stage develop in an outgoing spiral in a distinctive, Fibonacci pattern. We see this in his photos of dahlias and other members of the daisy family Asteraceae. Secondly, he loves those stems that terminate in a wheel of umbrella-like spokes. By altering light and perspective, these stems come to remind us of the self-repeating patterns associated with traditional French lace and landscapes in knot garlands. Instead of someone weaving them into gardens, joSon shows they are garlands.

Collectors may find themselves comparing joSon's work to that of a more recent master of domestic flower portraits, Robert Mapplethorpe. There are a few similarities. Both enjoy the diversity available in a commercial, American, greenhouse. Both would also probably agree that a studio photo of a domesticated flower says far more about the personal and private choices of the photographer than it does about how humans alter trends in plant evolution.

From there, their art diverges. Because joSon embraces color, you can't say that his flowers have the "black edge" Mapplethorpe believed he gave his blooms. The tropical plants preferred by Mapplethorpe descend from species that evolved a thick, protective, waxy cuticle retarding evaporation and damage by ultra-violet light under an unforgiving sun. Mapplethorpe delighted in showing how light bounced off these cuticles leading to some startling images. joSon's photos, meanwhile, do not startle as much as they redefine. His use of light shows how Nature, and man's selective breeding, induces repeatable patterns. Think of any flowering branch or flower as a module in which symmetry is based on a program of repetition. For plants, repetition is the rule, not the exception. That is why joSon's remarkable photos of florets in dahlia head or the fringed tips of a tulip may remind you of the scaled hide of a reptile or the fluted edges of some sea creature's shell.

The end result may seem, to some, otherworldly. I showed these photos to a friend recently and she complained, "They're too perfect." That's a good thing. Domesticated flowers are not about life in the wild. They're about choices we make after preceding generations make choices. joSon makes a choice to use modern techniques to return to an earlier age. He wants depth and detail with his bouquet.

PETER BERNHARDT, PROFESSOR OF BOTANY
Department of Biology. St.Louis University, St. Louis, MO

Foreword by

Peter Bernhardt

Botanical editing

Frank Almeda

Horticultural research by

Paul Lee Cannon

THIS BOOK IS DEDICATED

John Woods

Sanh Van Lee

Maureen Cronin

Neal & Aida Nicholas

Pat Leonard-Heffener

Flowers have always spoken the language of our senses. Time and again we struggle to find those images which can best express our innermost emotions, and yet it seems that the language we've learned to depend on fails us. A single flower can often fill in that void, conveying an illumination only the heart can understand. Not surprisingly, flowers' connection to mankind can be traced back as far as our earliest prehistoric cave paintings. But as leading botanist and popular science writer William Burger pointed out in his book *Flowers: How They Changed the World*, the connection between humans and flowers is even more fundamental. Burger explains: "Since they energize themselves by capturing the energy of sunlight, flowers provide a vital link in the chain of life. Even today in our complex technological world, it is the flowering plants that provide us, directly or indirectly, with nearly all the energy that sustains life." He goes on to say, "Without flowers, we humans simply wouldn't be here, whether as primates, two-legged omnivores, or grand civilizations!" Long after our human civilizations have crumbled, the

flowers—from Tulips to Roses, Magnolias to Camellias, Orchids to Irises — will still carry within them a snapshot of our own time here. Their gorgeous colors, intriguing forms, unique textures and their brief lifespan are like a lost civilization that draws me inward and compels me to document their lives, until all that remains is one central question: how do flowers play such a crucial role in our human cultures and emotions? Which came first …the human need for flowers, or the power of the flowers themselves to evoke and enhance and call forth those same emotions from us through light and color and scent? If the flower is just an innocent plant, why do they have the power to bring so much of love, joy, solace and memory into our lives? Perhaps then what I'm showing here is not so much the portraits of flowers but portraits of our own souls — because through them we learn more about ourselves, our own emotions, and how we meld and melt into the world around us.

INTIMATE PORTRAITS OF NATURE

$\mathcal{D}$AHLIA 22

Mum Chrysanthemum 25

Teacup Flower 32

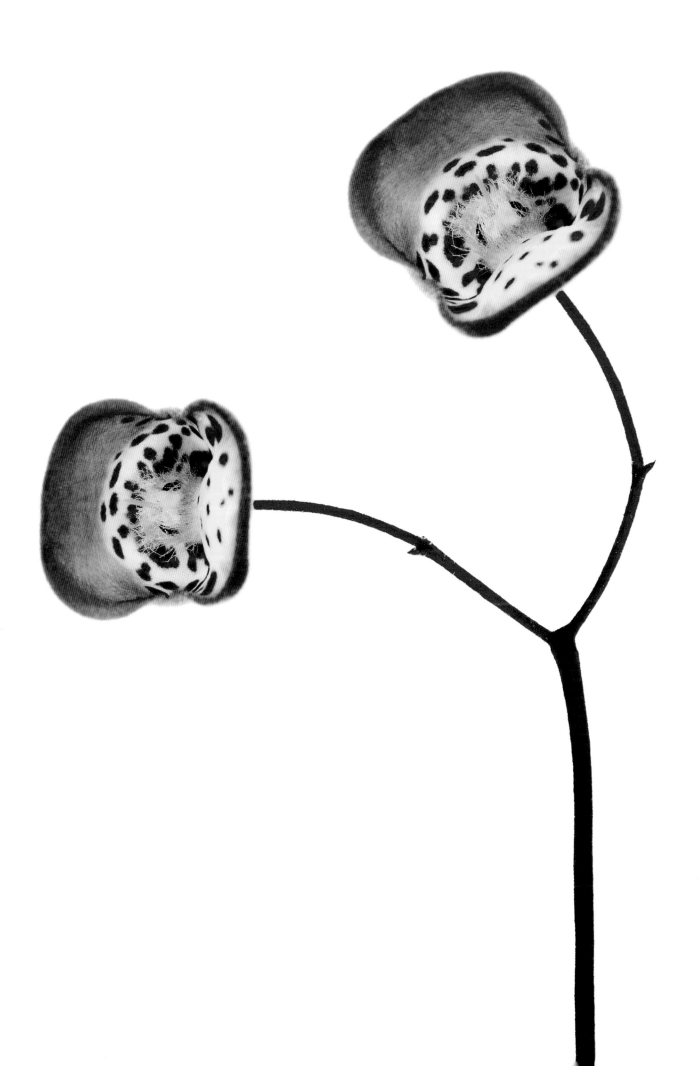

Dahlia 36

Torch Ginger 38

Lily-of-the-Nile 50

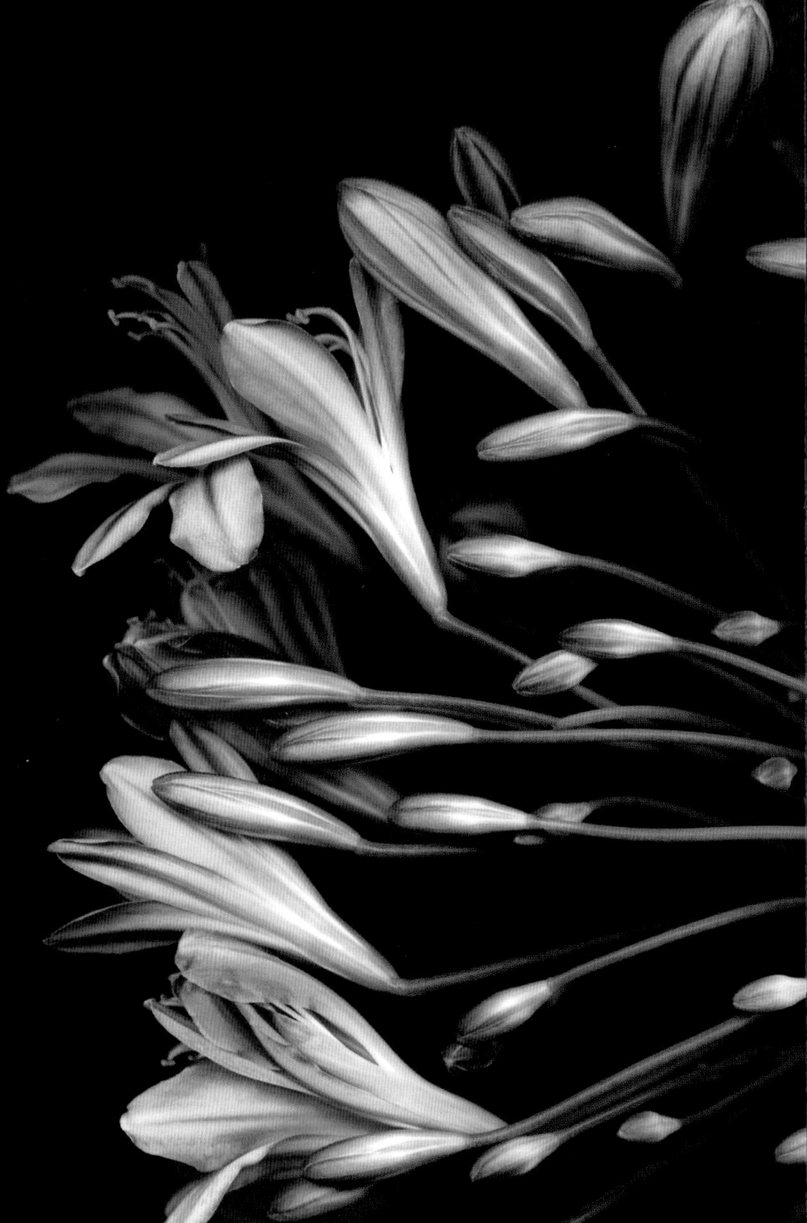

African Daisy 56

Blue Puya 60

BLUE DAWN FLOWER 64

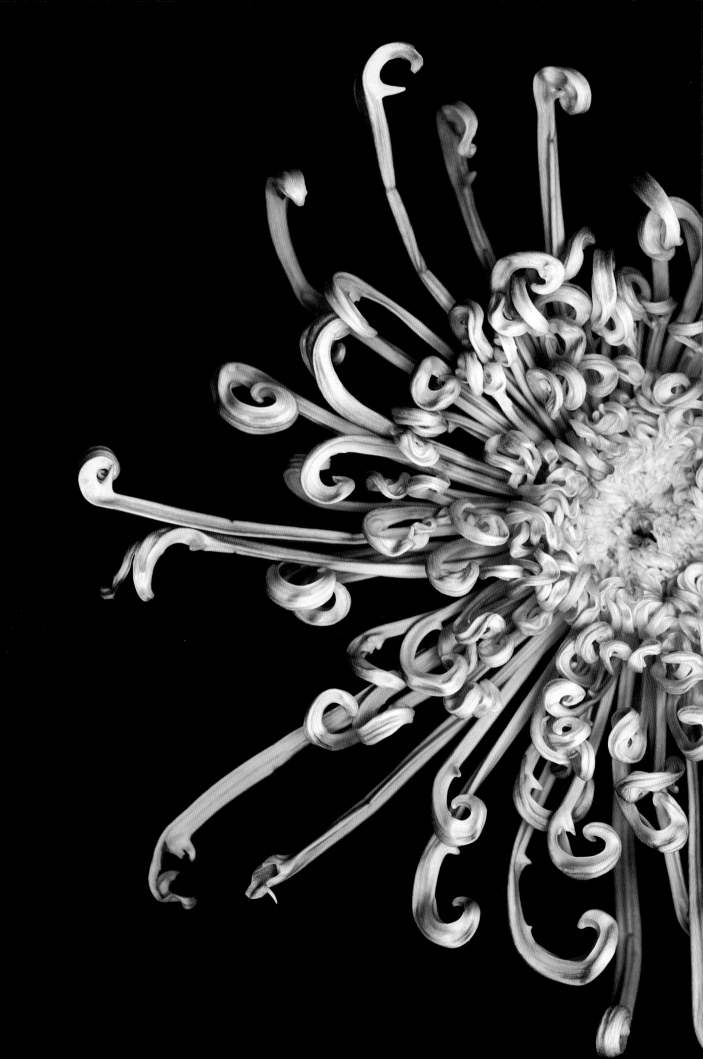

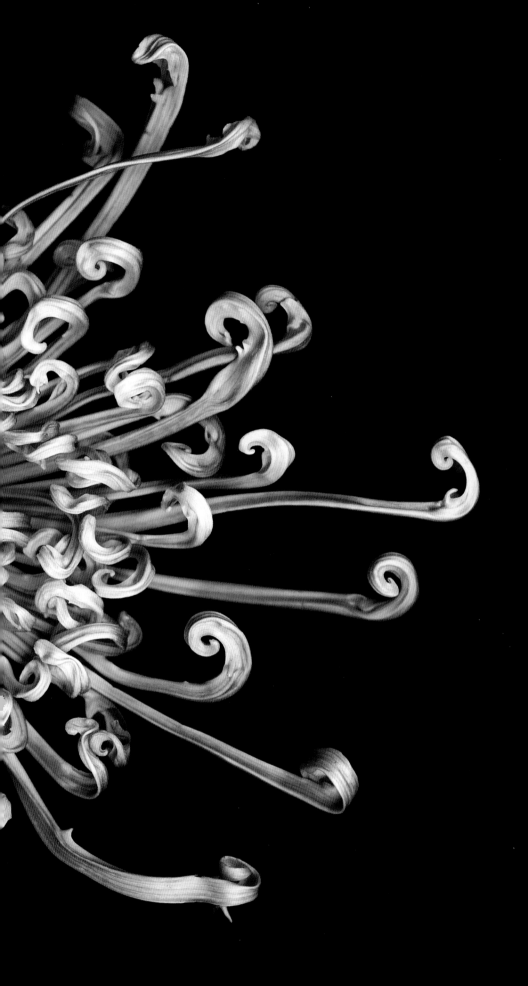

Spider Chrysanthemum 67

Fabio Tulip 68

Lactea 'Cristat' 72

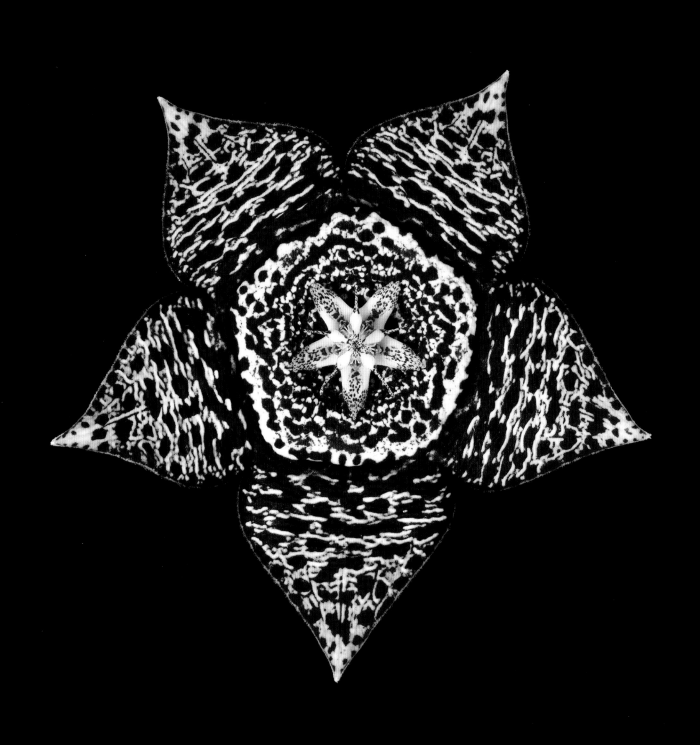

Dahlia 76

Iris 77

Abu Hassan Tulip 79

*M*ATILIJA POPPY 80

ORIENTAL POPPY 82

Rose 85

FLAMINGO FLOWER 86

Lycaste Orchid 91

Imschoot's Renanthera Orchid 92

Cymbidium Orchid 94

Wisteria sinensis 96

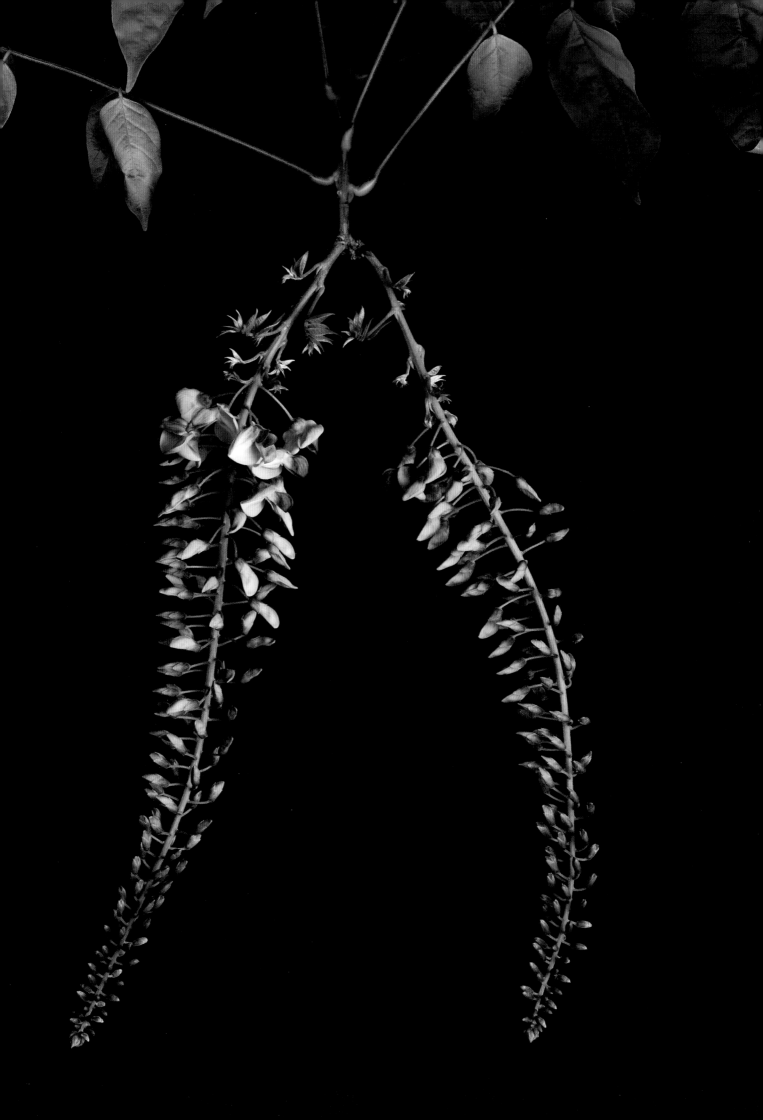

Epiphyllum Hybrid 100

GREEN TRICK CARNATION 110

CORAL ALOE 112

Monkey Hand Tree 116

White Calla Lily 118

Costa Rican Butterfly Vine 122

COLUMBINE 124

Large-Flowered Cyrtochilum Orchid 132

White Triumphator Tulip 135

CHAPARE MASDEVALLIA ORCHID 142

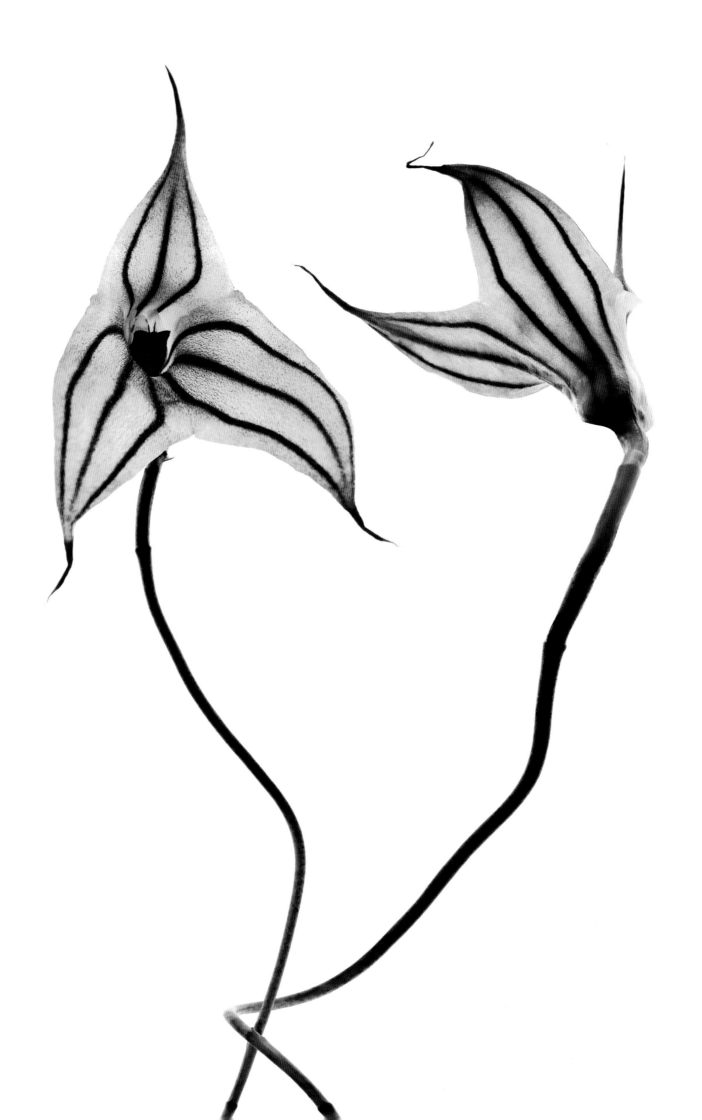

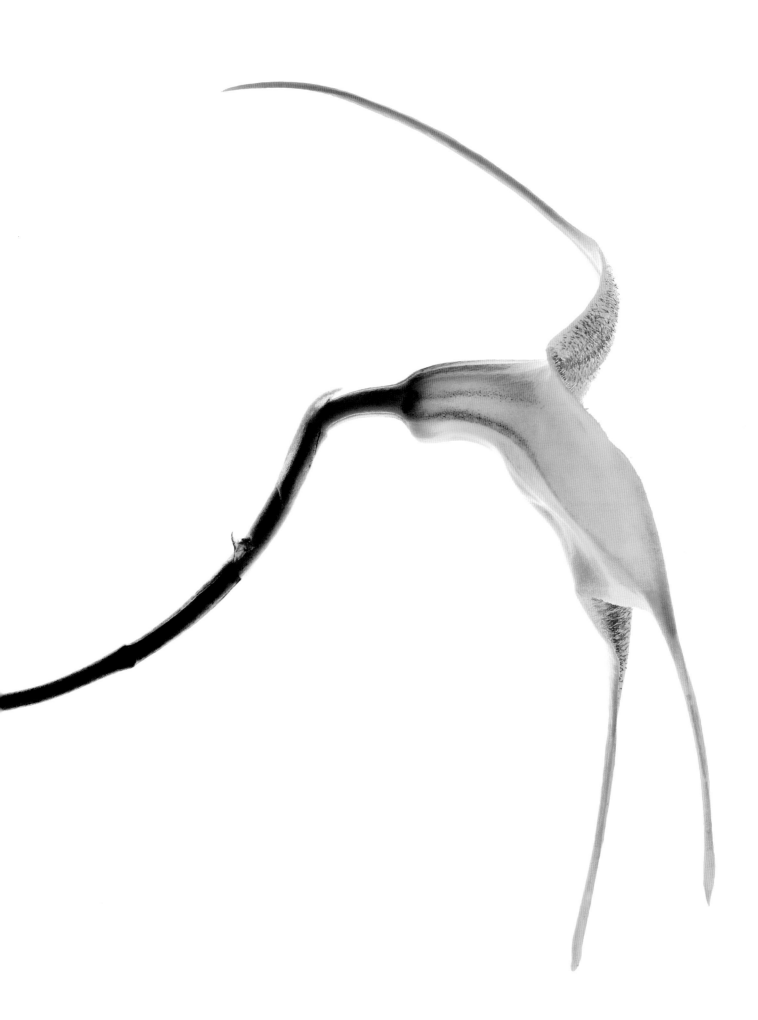

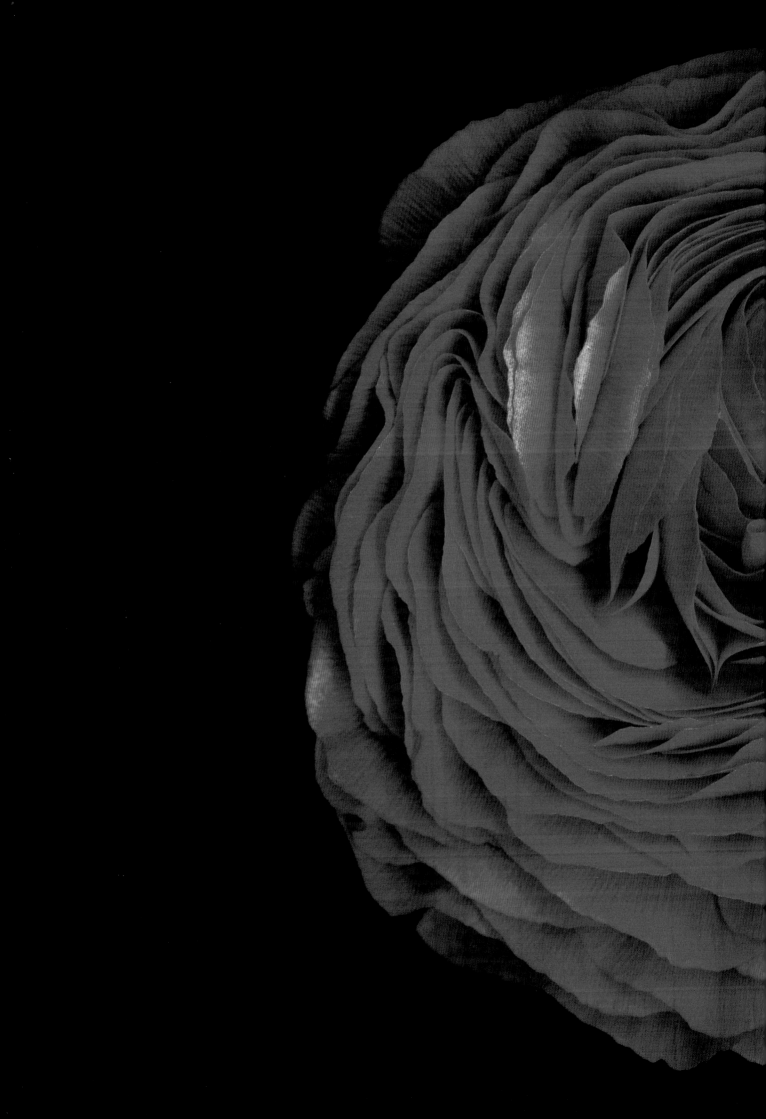

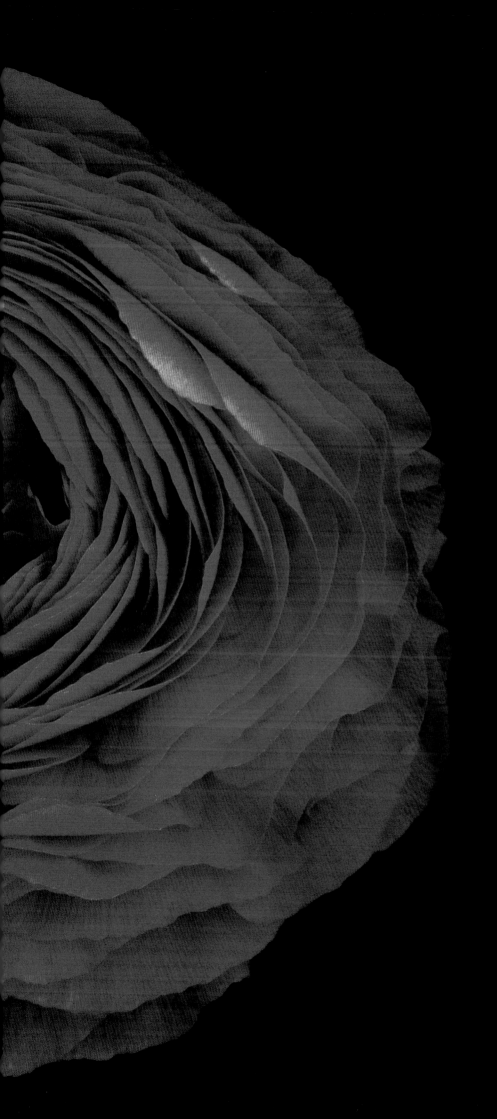

Apricot Parrot Tulip 156

Orange Roses 158

Flaming Parrot Tulip 166

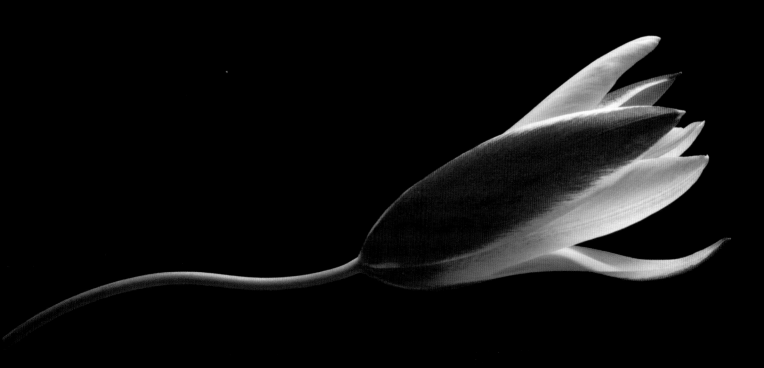

Purple Pitcher Plant 172

White Caucasian Pincushion 172

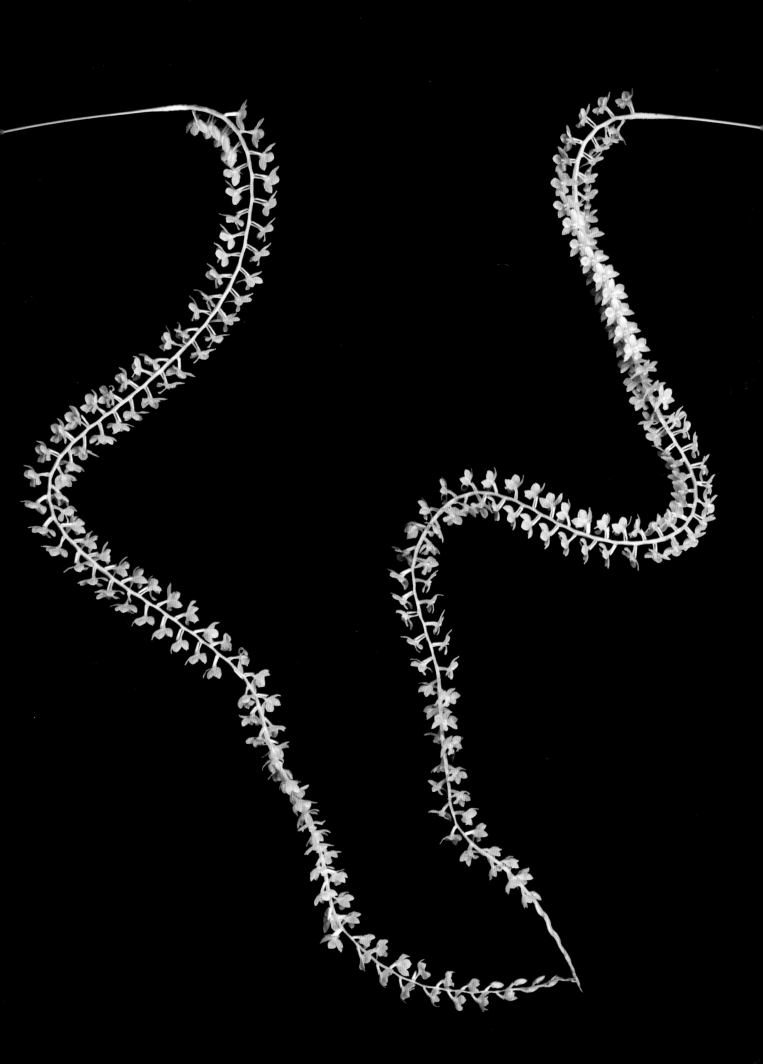

Flamingo Queen Begoni 180

Maja Tulip 183

New Design & Salmon Parrot Tulip 184

Ballerina Tulip 194

Magnolia 198

ndex

CKNOWLEDGEMENTS

SPECIAL THANKS

Frank Almeda

Peter Bernhardt

Mark F. Bonner

Paul Cannon

Don Cravalho

Brent Dennis

Tuan Huynh

Scott Lankford

David Le

Jimin Nam

Tuan Nguyen

Martin Pedersen

Tom Perlite

Brent Roozen

Sandip Roy

Ming Tsang

Chris Young

Orchid, Tulip and Epiphyllum
Collections are provided by

RoozenGaarde
Mount Vermon, Washington.
www.tulips.com

Golden Gate Orchids,
San Francisco, California
www.goldengateorchids.com

Epiphyllum World
www.epiphyllumworld.com

Additional samples of the
flowers are also available:
The San Francisco Botanical Garden
and The Conservatory of Flowers,
Golden Gate Park, San Francisco, California
www.golden-gate-park.com

Tools and Equipment:
All the images were captured by
either digital camera
or by placing the flower directly
on a flatbed scanner.

camera and lens: Canon
scanner: Epson
lighting : Profoto
software: Adobe Photoshop

Images, Introduction and Information are copyrighted © 2013 joSon Nicholas-Lee and joSon Photo LLC.

All contents in this book are copyrighted by joSon Nicholas-Lee/joSon Photo LLC. All rights reserved.
No portion of this book may be reproduced, stored in a retrieval system, or transmitted in any form or any means,
mechanical, electronic, photocopying, recording, or otherwise, without written permission from the copyright holder.

This book is available at special discounts when purchased in quantity for premiums and promotions as well as
fundraising or educational use. Special editions can also be created to specification.
For details, please contact Graphis or the photographer's Studio.

Image licensing and permission write to:
email: joson@joSonstudio.com,
Phone: 1. 510. 653. 1194, 1. 917. 673 0098. joSon Studio.
1121 40th Street, Suite 2201, Emeryville Ca. 94608

Printed and bound in China

or write to joSon@joSonstudio.com.

1. 917. 673 0098

All images in this book are available in limited edition prints,
for more information please visit: www.josonstudio.com
or write to joSon@joSonstudio.com.
1. 917. 673 0098